# The 3x5 Coach

# The 3x5 Coach

A PRACTICAL GUIDE TO COACHING YOUR TEAM
FOR GREATER RESULTS AND HAPPIER PEOPLE

Dave Baney

ANSWERS GROW YOUR BUSINESS

55 Questions, LLC
PO Box 401522
Las Vegas, NV 89140

www.55questions.com

ISBN: 1544825323
ISBN-13: 9781544825328

# Contents

# Testimonials

*"If you want to improve your game as an employee, coach, or leader or in starting a new business, read this book! Dave Baney has distilled what is found in thousands of business books into a practical, methodical, and most important, implementable series of steps. Dave teaches how to slow down so you can accelerate your business's growth by aligning teams, building commitment to the plan and delivering results."*

Les Rubenovitch
President, Winning Edge Consultants Inc.

*"Dave Baney has outlined a practical, simple-to-understand-and-follow process that will contribute to the success of any size organization from a start-up to a Fortune 500 company. Buy it, follow it, and be successful!"*

Bill McIlwaine
Executive Director at Tri-Kids Inc.

*"Employees must know the answers to two fundamental yet rarely asked questions that drive accountability and performance: "What do I get paid to accomplish or produce?"*

(accountability) and "How will I be measured against that?" (performance). Both are routinely absent, overcomplicated, and/or under communicated. Managers wonder why performance is subpar, and employees wonder why their managers don't give them more clarity. Sound frustratingly familiar? Dave Baney has the solution: a straightforward, practical process that not only helps managers and employees answer both questions clearly but also facilitates execution, getting things done as planned. If you're serious about growing your business and if you're in need of a simple, actionable process to help align your organization, this is the book for you."

Mark E. Green
President, Performance Dynamics Group LLC

"Dave Baney is the Vince Lombardi of CEO coaches. His approach involves asking questions and then more questions, some of which are uncomfortable to answer. Who's accountable for that? Why is this box in the O-chart empty? What happens if this deadline is missed? This book, like Dave's techniques, offers help that is wise, tested, and 100 percent practical."

Bob Killian, Killian Branding

"Clear direction is such a critical component of leadership, yet so many of us seem to skip steps as we run from one task to the next. In his book, Dave Baney, a.k.a. Mr. Accountability, provides simple tools and tips that really work. It helped us transition the business into its next generation and restructure the company to appropriately reflect its actual size."

Jonathan Padnos
President of PADNOS, Recycling the world over, and over®

"Coaching has replaced the traditional role of managing. This book lays out a practical and straightforward method for coaching members of your team as well as planning for future organizational needs."

Verne Harnish

Author of *Scaling Up (Rockefeller Habits 2.0)*, *The Greatest Business Decisions of All Time*, and *Mastering the Rockefeller Habits*

"The 3x5 Coach is the secret weapon of business books when it comes to building high-growth companies. This actionable methodology quickly achieves clarity between the leader and employee on their accountabilities and performance measures aligned to a discussed and agreed-upon plan. This book is a great reflection of Dave's proven and practical insights, methods, and tools that have made him a highly effective coach to other business leaders. This is a must-read for every business leader and coach looking to take it to the next level."

Shannon Byrne Susko

Serial Entrepreneur/CEO Coach/Speaker

Amazon best-selling author of *The Metronome Effect: The Journey to Predictable Profit*

"Wayne Gretzky once said, 'A good hockey player plays where the puck is. A great hockey player plays where the puck is going to be.' The same is true with Dave and business. He can see three steps ahead to where your business is headed and give you the tools to get there. The 3x5 Coach is pure Dave in that regard: loaded with ideas and tools to position your team and your business for where it is headed.

This book is practical, actionable, and just what leaders of growing businesses need. Keep it handy; you'll be reaching for it often."

Maureen Berkner Boyt

Head Moxie at The Moxie Exchange

"For those looking to simplify their approach to building an organization, Dave Baney gives a simple low-tech process that is sure to help you understand and apply big-picture thinking."

Kevin Daum

*Inc. Magazine* columnist and author of *Video Marketing For Dummies*

"Dave parlays his decades of business experience and shares his insights in an easy-to-read book which is insightful yet concise. Having organizational consistency within a business or a team is an area many struggle with regularly. The 3x5 Coach lays out an easy-to-follow road map for those wanting to develop coaching skills and build alignment. A quick, enjoyable read that if executed, can add great value to any organization or team."

Craig Ahrens

Partner, FUNGO Consulting and author of *No Bad Team*

"I love the simplicity of The 3 x 5 Coach tool; it makes an impact and reminds leaders and their people of the most important thing we often forget: what we are all paid for. You made it simple and easy...a real back-to-basics approach that creates value for the business with clarity for the leader and their team.

*It's great that there is not an app, so that the employees and their supervisors have to talk to each other. This book is truly a how-to book that is straightforward to execute in any organization with immediate improvement in communication and focus for the leadership and team members."*

Kevin Lawrence
Adviser to CEOs and executive teams
www.LawrenceandCo.com

# Foreword

Occasionally in our lives, we encounter seasoned colleagues in business who become friends and mentors because of their life experience, skills, and heart. Author, friend, and mentor Dave Baney has been this type of gift in my life over the past six-plus years as I have led Gazelles International Coaching Association.

During seasons of amazing growth; short periods of grueling difficulty; and the mundane, steady-state times, Dave has provided keen insights and wisdom based on taking the long view of business (and life), and has developed tools and techniques that he has abundantly shared throughout our community of more than two hundred coaches on six continents.

It is from his decades of business and now coaching experience that he gives to each of us *The 3 x 5 Coach*.

*The 3 x 5 Coach* is a simple, practical, and actionable set of principles and tools that any business leader can use to address one of the most challenging recurring problems I see through the eyes of our coaches worldwide: providing focus, clarity, and effective coaching to employees in an easy, scalable manner, regardless of company size, industry, or employee functional role.

In our age of technology, virtual meetings, and non-real-time communication, *The 3 x 5 Coach* restores the simple human touch to the leader–direct report relationship through the simplicity of a 3 x 5 card, a limited number of job accountabilities, and regular coaching.

Enjoy the gift he has provided us and the refreshing simplicity that makes it great.

Keith Cupp
CEO, Gazelles International Coaching Association
www.GICoaches.com

# Acknowledgments

*T*he *3 x 5 Coach* came about as a result of years of coaching franchisees at Burger King and McDonald's Corporations as well as my own clients after leaving those two organizations. The need I saw in the business community is how to distinguish between what the "manager's" expectations were and what the employee's understanding of the job was.

This is fundamentally where most of those one-on-one relationships break down. It is a communication issue that exists because job descriptions have become legal documents more than they describe what an employee is to do, and it is compounded by today's seeming need for short and quick communication.

Rarely will you find supervisor and employee on the same page when it comes to expectations and performance.

And yet it is so simple to resolve and requires only that each party participate with a little preplanning and then a short conversation leading to agreement on why the employee gets paid and how that performance will be measured.

I have been teaching this method to my clients and fellow coaches for years and finally decided to share it with a broader audience because of their encouragement.

I would like to thank a number of people who influenced me over the years, who in fact have been the inspiration for this book, starting with Mike Granto, Kevin Moriarty, Don Dempsey, and Paul Clayton, plus all the people I had the privilege to work for and with at Burger King Corporation. Additionally, I'd like to thank Jack Greenberg, Charlie Bell, Ed Sanchez, and Claire Babrowski and the folks I had the privilege to work for and with at McDonald's Corporation. Some of these folks were truly great examples of leadership and coaching, while others were examples of management. I thank them all for the lessons I learned at their hands.

For ten years I was a franchisee of the Renaissance Executive Forums system and learned many fundamentals about sales and coaching there. Though much of the learning comes from the sharing of wisdom and lessons learned among peers (as in most organizations), I would like to thank Maureen Berkner Boyt, Ed Breclaw, Bill McIlwaine, Tony Hutti, Rick Johnson, Ken Keller, Walt Hardenstine, and Lee Self for being those special few who were always there.

Since 2009 I have been a coach with the Gazelles International Coaches organization, which honored me as a senior coach and member of the President's Advisory Board in 2012. I would like to acknowledge Verne Harnish for his thought leadership within Gazelles and Keith Cupp for providing me the opportunity to be a part the organization and for his leadership and mentoring over these past few years. I am truly grateful.

There are so many incredible coaches within the Gazelles International Coaching Association who have provided their time and knowledge in helping me to become a better coach; among them are Mark Green, Ron Huntington, Les Rubenovitch, Paul O'Kelly, Shannon Susko, David Carter, and Kevin Lawrence. Many thanks to each of you.

I would also like to thank all the clients I worked with during those years; it was truly an honor to work with and learn from each of you.

A lot of what gets done at 55 Questions wouldn't get done without the help and support of Wendy Swing. We have worked together for the past seven years. Wendy is a virtual assistant living over 1,500 miles away, and I have never known Wendy to miss a deadline, turn a project down, or not complete a project with the end result being beyond my expectations. I am very lucky to have been introduced to Wendy seven years ago.

As is the case for many of us, I had many lessons to learn while growing up. My parents did an amazing job of raising three kids; stretching a dollar; and teaching us the value of work and education, never in a harsh or heavy-handed way but always with a sense of knowing right from wrong.

Every day I am thankful for the love, guidance, and support of my wife, Nanette. Without her, most of what I have accomplished over these past years would not have been imaginable.

—Dave Baney

# CHAPTER 1

# The 3 x 5 Coach

D oes each member of your team know why he or she gets paid? In other words, how well are your employees' accountabilities defined?

Do you and your team members have the same understanding of why they get paid and what their top five accountabilities are? Are you sure?

Most people are presented with a job description at some point during their employment, and on occasion, the employee and supervisor even spend some time reviewing it. Most job descriptions are about two pages long and include a laundry list of duties that usually ends with "and other duties that may arise from time to time."

The job description is, in fact, usually a legal document that describes the requirements for continued employment, as opposed to a document designed to help the employee understand exactly what is expected of him or her in a new role. Among its many listed duties and accountabilities, which are the most important from your perspective, from your team member's perspective, and to the company this quarter and this year?

**Without some sense of clarity between employee and supervisor, it is easy to see how one person can be very happy with the team member's performance, while the other is very disappointed.**

Further, it is easy to see that without specific definition around the goals (e.g., how much, how many, how often, and so on), even if the two people involved agree on accountabilities, there can still be a difference of opinion on performance based on measured results versus expectations.

Rarely do job descriptions include metrics around performance. Without metrics, how does one know if goals are being met or if performance is up to expectations?

It doesn't have to be this way. **Instead of managing or supervising, behave like a coach.** A good coach guides and supports each member of his or her team to maximize the performance of the individuals and for the team results.

Let's start with the cliché of everyone being on the same team. In sports, the coach and the members of the team know they are on the same team. They can tell by their uniforms and which side of the field they are on. But in business, there are times when the coach and the team members can seem not to be on the same team: they are not aligned.

The 3 x 5 coach is always aligned with his or her team. All participants know the goals and accountabilities, because they have discussed them and agreed upon them; as a result, they have clarity and a common understanding, without confusion or second-guessing.

The team members all understand their own roles and know what the coach expects, so they are each free to address their top five accountabilities with the confidence that comes from knowing what is expected and because there are performance measurements or key performance indicators (KPIs) attached to each accountability.

The employees know how well they are performing at all times. The workplace is definitely happier when its direction and goals are clear and level of performance is openly measured.

## Trust And Communication Are Hallmarks Of Great Coaching.

Here are dictionary definitions of manager and coach. Note the differences.

### Manager
noun

- a person who has control or direction of an institution, business, etc., or of a part, division, or phase of it.
- a person who controls and manipulates resources and expenditures, as of a household.

## Coach
noun

- a person who trains an athlete or a team of athletes: a football coach.
- a private tutor who prepares a student for an examination.
- a person who instructs an actor or singer.

verb

- to give instruction or advice to, in the capacity of a coach; instruct:

Whom would you rather work with?

# CHAPTER 2

# The 3 x 5 Card

Using two very high-tech tools, an index card (a three-inch-by-five-inch card referred to as the 3 x 5 Card once implemented) and a two-inch-by-two-inch Post-it Super Sticky Note (referred to as the *Post-it Note*), you can develop a simple but powerful accountability and alignment system.

I recommend you use white, unruled 3 x 5 cards and a pale-colored Post-it Super Sticky Note. As an organization, choose black or blue ink so that there is a consistent look to all of your completed 3 x 5 Cards. This will be beneficial later when you do organization planning and individual development. (I'll discuss these later.)

The reason for keeping this process simple and using pen and paper instead of an app or online tool is that the real value of the tool is in the communication between coach and each team member. An online tool would allow the coach and team member to use a text message or e-mail version of this communication process, which defeats the whole purpose: pairs of people having goal-setting conversations live, face-to-face or, at the very least, virtually face-to-face.

Separately, the coach and team member are to complete this exercise and then schedule time to meet and compare their views.

Here's an example of a completed 3 x 5 Card, both front and back:

**Front of Card**

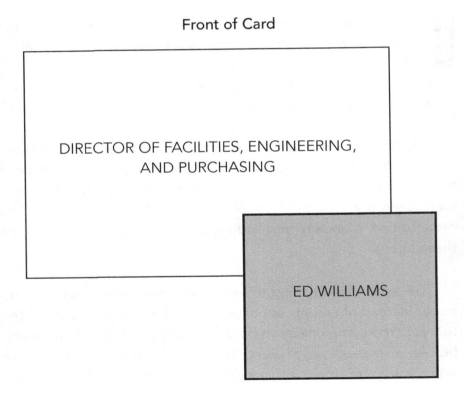

DIRECTOR OF FACILITIES, ENGINEERING, AND PURCHASING

ED WILLIAMS

Back of Card

## WHY DO YOU GET PAID?

- Complete all approved facilities projects on budget and on time: +/- 5% of budget and finished on time or early
- Reduce energy consumption by 5% through facility and engineering improvements
- Maximize revenue generation by developing prioritized-capital spending plan that enhances revenue growth +3%
- Achieve internal customer satisfaction score of +60% using the Net Promoter System* for evaluation of performance
- All purchase invoices paid within 30 days of receipt

- Read at least one book per month
- Learn to play the piano

Here is the process the coach and team member each will follow:

- Start with a blank 3 x 5 card.
- On the front of the card, write the position title. Do **not** include the person's name.
- On the back of the card, write the *top five reasons* a person holding this position gets paid. These are the person's

five accountabilities. Rank them in order from most to least important.

- Next to each of the accountabilities, write a metric for performance measurement so that performance may be objectively evaluated.

By now, you see why I recommend a 3 x 5 card. **It has a very limited amount of space, so you must choose only five accountabilities. Be clear in your thinking about what the team member must do and how you will measure his or her performance.**

So, ask yourself: What does a person in a particular role contribute to the success of the organization? Which of his or her contributions are the most important, and how do we measure the impact of those contributions?

That is why we put five monosyllabic words—*Why do you get paid?*—at the top on the back side of the 3 x 5 Card. *(Brief)*

- **How exactly do you earn your paycheck?** In other words...
- **What is the real purpose of your role?** In other words...
- **What is the real value that your position brings to the organization?**

Once you have settled on the top five reasons, then the measurements can usually be best determined by another simple question: "How do you know if you are doing a good job?"

As the leader of the organization, start with yourself. Create a 3 x 5 Card for your position. Find someone else to do one for you as well, whether it is a board of directors, your executive coach, or maybe someone from a professional organization you belong to who knows you well.

Now, have a one-on-one with your "coach" to finalize your 3 x 5 Card.

Next, move on to the leadership team. As the organization's leader, complete your direct reports' 3 x 5 Cards first and have your one-on-one meetings to finalize their cards with you as their coach.

The next step is to cascade the process through the rest of the organization.

It will take a while for some people to grasp the concept of accountabilities versus tasks. It will also be a challenge for some people to limit themselves to only five accountabilities. By far the most challenging part, though, is quantifying or measuring performance.

Many times I have been told, "You don't understand. My position is unique, and most of what I do can't be measured."

My response is direct and simple: "What would you say if I told you, 'If there are no KPIs, there is no job'?" This usually causes people to rethink their "it can't be measured" position and, amazingly, come up with a few good ways to document performance.

Stick with it. Almost everything any of us do can be defined in a way that allows us to develop KPIs.

Once the 3 x 5 Card is complete, stick a Post-it Note to the lower-right corner of the card so that most of the Post-it Note hangs below it.

Next, the team member will do these two things:

- Write his or her name on the front of the Post-it Note.
- Write one or two things on the back of the Post-it Note that he or she will do this year for personal growth. (These must be visible on the Post-it Note while it is attached to the 3 x 5 Card.)

The one or two items each team member wants to accomplish for personal growth this year are just that: personal and for their growth. These items may or may not be work related. Goals may include travel, learning to play an instrument, getting an advanced degree, reading, improving a golf handicap, or any other personal interests or work-related growth goals. All are acceptable.

**The Post-it Note is all about the team member. Each can choose his or her own areas for personal growth.** Once a commitment to personal growth is made, the coach should treat that the same as a commitment to achieve work-related goals and continue to inquire about each team member's progress toward it.

**The purpose for the coach's follow-up is to provide support and gentle pressure toward the achievement of personal goals.** Team members' job performance should not, however, be judged by their achievement (or not) of their personal goals—only by their work accountabilities.

**The reason the team member's name does not go on the 3 x 5 Card is that the card is about the position, not the person.** Plus, if the team member's name is on the 3 x 5 Card, then it is harder to remove the team member from the position, so how can he or she get promoted?

The Post-it Note is about the person, not the position; that is why it has the team member's name and personal growth goals on it. It is all about the team member, and it can easily be removed from the current 3 x 5 Card and moved to another card if there is a need for organizational change.

*But we are not done.*

While the team member does a 3 x 5 Card for his or her current position, so does the coach. Once both have completed these cards, it is time for the two parties to meet.

Each of them will bring their version of the 3 x 5 Card to the meeting. There will be blank 3 x 5 cards and Post-it Notes in the meeting room as well. The purpose of the meeting is for both parties to share everything they've written about the position on their cards and then discuss the title, role, top five reasons a person in this position gets paid, and how to evaluate each of those accountabilities until they agree on all points and can jointly write a single new 3 x 5 Card for the position.

Once the new card is complete, both the coach and team member will have a copy, complete with a Post-it Note, for future and frequent reference.

Now, and maybe for the first time in each team member's career, they can be confident that they are focused on the right things and know where they stand at all times because of the performance metrics.

*The Net Promoter System (NPS) is a measure of customer satisfaction developed by Fred Reichheld. His book *The Ultimate Question 2.0* provides an in-depth review of the process. There is a corollary to the Net Promoter System, known as eNPS, which measures employee satisfaction in the same manner as NPS measures customer satisfaction.

- This is the key question from the NPS system: "How likely is it that you would recommend *Company Name / Product / Service* to a friend or colleague?" (Respondents answer on a zero-to-ten scale.)
- This is the key question from the eNPS system: "How likely is it that you would recommend *Company Name* to a friend as a great place to work?" (Answers here are also on a zero-to-ten scale.)

# CHAPTER 3

# The Coaching Rhythm

Nobody wants to feel managed, but most people will gladly receive coaching. Coaching is a beneficial way of developing your team members' knowledge, skills, and abilities. It is also meant to boost team members' performance. When done regularly, it can help you, as the coach, to deal with any issues and challenges well before they become significant problems.

There was a time not so long ago that people were given annual performance reviews and an accompanying raise in pay. Thank goodness that at most companies today, team members don't have to wait a whole year to find out how they are doing.

A good coach meets with each team member on a weekly, monthly, and quarterly basis. Each meeting serves a specific purpose, but when taken as a whole, they create an ongoing dialogue about performance, issues, and challenges. This provides a team member the chance to seek advice and direction from the coach and for the coach to better understand the team member's thinking process.

A coaching session should be a scheduled conversation between the coach and the team member that focuses on helping the team member discover solutions for himself or herself. People generally are much more likely to embrace solutions they have come up with than solutions mandated by their managers.

**A good coach first looks at the behavior of the team member. Is he or she living the organization's core values?** If so, point out specific recent occurrences that stand out in your mind as great examples of living the core values. If not, point out specific recent occurrences when the core values were violated and discuss the issue with the team member. Ask him or her about the circumstance leading to the violation.

Next, a good coach looks at the achievement of goals, priorities, and activities that the team member committed to accomplish. Is the team member on track to perform to the agreed-upon levels? If so, point out specific positive outcomes that stand out in your mind. If not, point out specific outcomes that have fallen or are falling short and have the team member come up with the solution to get back on track.

There are a couple of last points to mention about these coaching meetings. First of all, when you are in a meeting (whether with your own coach or with a team member), *be there*. Don't let your mind wander off to some other issue or topic. Be focused—not reading e-mail, checking voice mail, taking phone calls, or engaging in any other rude behavior.

Once a meeting is scheduled, it should happen. **These are not meetings to be moved about freely.** If it is worth doing, it is worth doing right and with respect. It is easy to make the excuse that "something important has come up." What does that say to the other participant, that he or she is not important or that you don't respect their time?

So make time for your team members, and realize that it may be the most important twenty to thirty minutes of your day and theirs.

## The Weekly Update

On a weekly basis, the coach and team member should spend twenty to thirty minutes meeting face-to-face (if possible). During this time, the team member provides an update on his or her activities and accomplishments of the past week and also the game plan for the next week. This is **not a review of a calendar but of his or her accomplishments, goals, and priorities as well as the plan for the coming week.**

The meeting is an opportunity for the coach to ask about any issues or challenges the team member is facing, to talk about time management, and to listen to what the team member expresses regarding his or her concerns and successes (as well as how he or she communicates them).

Here are some questions to consider during these meetings:

- Are the assigned tasks and priorities getting the right amount of focus and effort?
- Is the team member encountering any roadblocks?
- If the employee is part of a work team, is the team working together well?

- Based on the current state of the team member's work, will all priorities and goals be accomplished this month and quarter? If not, what can be done to make that happen?
- Does the team member need any help?

This is also a good time to bring up any outstanding behavior that truly represents the spirit of the organization's core values (or any areas of behavioral concern regarding these values).

## The Monthly Review

On a monthly basis, the coach and team member should spend twenty to thirty minutes meeting face-to-face (if possible). The team member provides a **status update on his or her priorities and goals for the quarter.** Is each goal *green* (it will get done), *yellow* (it is in process, but there is some risk), or *red* (it is unlikely to be completed)?

This meeting replaces that week's Weekly Update session.

The meeting is an opportunity for the coach to ask about any issues or challenges the team member is facing, to talk about time management, and to listen to what the team member expresses regarding his or her concerns and successes (as well as how he or she communicates them).

As in the Weekly Update, you may want to consider the following for discussion:

- Are the assigned tasks and priorities getting the right amount of focus and effort?

- Is the team member encountering any roadblocks?
- If the employee is part of a work team, is the team working together well?
- Based on the current state of work, will all priorities and goals be accomplished this quarter? If not, what can be done to make that happen?
- Does the team member need any help?

## The Quarterly Recap

On a quarterly basis, the coach and team member should spend twenty to thirty minutes together **recapping the top five reasons the team member gets paid and the achievement status of the performance metrics for the quarter.**

Were the goals achieved? If they weren't, why not? What did the team member learn that he or she (and you) could apply moving forward?

The coach and team member should each provide a brief summary of their views of the team member's performance, including both the positives and the areas for improvement.

These short Quarterly Recaps are meant to keep both the coach and team member on the same page with respect to expectations for performance and level of satisfaction with the current level of performance. This way, there are no surprises for either person.

The Quarterly Recap does *not* replace the Monthly Review; it is an additional meeting.

Prior to the start of the next quarter, determine what the performance metric will be for each of the accountabilities for the upcoming quarter. Do any of the accountabilities need to be revised?

All of this can be accomplished in the given time frame if both parties come prepared for the discussion. Prior to the meeting, review the 3 x 5 Card and make note of the accountabilities and performance metrics. Reflect on the performance and the achievement of the goals as defined by the metrics (the what) as well as the way in which the work was done (the *how*).

- Is there a trail of unhappy employees, customers, or suppliers?
- Did it appear that there was a plan to accomplish the quarter's goals?
- Were the company's assets used properly in pursuit of the goals?
- Were the goals achieved with grace under pressure and with a positive attitude?

The purpose of the Quarterly Recap is to ensure regular and frequent discussion of not just what was achieved but also how it was achieved. Coaching to help the team member become more successful is the goal. So as a coach, be supportive, honest, and constructive with the team member.

Together, discuss the ways that the accountabilities could have been achieved more efficiently and more effectively, and listen for ideas about how the work can be done differently in the future.

Many organizations have a formal review process. The Quarterly Recap is a supplement to that process, to improve communication and build on current successes.

## What If The Coach And Team Member Don't Agree On The Performance? How Does That Get Resolved?

The beauty of having five accountabilities and each of the five measured by a KPI is that discussion of them should be relatively black-and-white when it comes to achievement: Were the goals met or not?

This is business, not horseshoes, so "close" is not a measure of success. Both parties agreed on a number, percentage, or time frame. Were the goals achieved? It is a simple question to answer.

But what about extenuating circumstances? The coach and the team member should not wait until the Quarterly Recap to discuss any special circumstances that may affect the company's ability to achieve the goals.

Part of everyone's job is not only to accomplish their goals and priorities but also to anticipate potential issues and, when necessary, adjust to changing circumstances.

Performance and achievement of goals should be relatively easy to discuss. What may be a bit harder and less clear-cut to define are the effort and method required to achieve the goals.

If circumstances dictate that the Quarterly Recap needs to be longer than twenty to thirty minutes for thorough discussion and to have both parties come to agreement, then take the extra time to do it right. After all, this process is about good coaching and communication.

But with these weekly, monthly, and quarterly meetings, how is the coach able to do his or her own work?

## The Role Of The Coach Is To Get Things Done By Using The Skills And Talents Of The Team As Well As To Train And Grow The Team Members' Skills. How Can A Coach Accomplish All This Without Spending Time With The People He Or She Coaches?

Even if a coach has ten direct reports and spends thirty minutes per week with each team member that is only five hours per week.

If the same coach spends an additional thirty minutes with each team member every month, that is only five hours per month.

Finally, if that coach were to spend thirty minutes with each team member every quarter that requires an additional five hours per quarter.

Now for a quick look at the math of coaching: with ten direct reports each having a thirty-minute Weekly Update, the coach would spend *sixty-five* hours over a three-month period (10 people x 30 minutes each x 13 weeks).

With ten direct reports each having a thirty-minute Monthly Review, the coach would spend *fifteen* hours over a three-month period (10 people x 30 minutes each x 3 months). Remember, these each replace a Weekly Update, so this time does not get added to the total.

Finally, with ten direct reports each having a thirty-minute Quarterly Recap, the coach would spend *five* hours over a three-month period (10 people x 30 minutes each x 1 quarter).

This is a total of seventy hours over the course of thirteen weeks. Most managers (who are hopefully becoming tomorrow's coaches) tell me they work forty-five to fifty hours per week. So the coach with ten direct reports who follows this process will spend about 15 percent of his or her working time each quarter coaching team members. (Again, this assumes ten direct reports.)

So much can be accomplished using less than 15 percent of the coach's time. **Research shows that most employees quit their coaches, not the company.**

## Stop Managing, And Start Coaching Your Team Members Regularly!
This will reduce turnover and increase productivity on your team. What could be more important?

Note: If you would like to take coaching a step further, take a look at "Peer Coaching Overview," by Dr. Marshall Goldsmith, Andrew Thorn, and Marilyn McLeod from 2007. They offer great insights into the value of peer-to-peer coaching.

# CHAPTER 4

# Recruiting and Interviewing

By using the top five reasons a team member gets paid and metrics from the 3 x 5 Card, you should have clarity when recruiting to fill an open position. You know what you are looking for and should be able to clearly state it in any advertising or job posting.

Develop a scorecard for the position that includes a stated *purpose for the role*, why this job exists, in one or two sentences. Next, list the top five accountabilities. Then add seven to ten *critical competencies* of the ideal team member. Finally, include the organization's core values—this will help determine if the candidate is the right fit for the organization, not just the position.

You'll use this scorecard when hiring. It provides the staff members involved in the interviewing and hiring process a common understanding and assures that everyone looks at the position in the same way.

Now you are ready to begin the process of recruiting prospective candidates.

When you define the purpose of the role and its top five accountabilities, prospective candidates can better self-select for the open position or opt out, thus giving the recruiting person a better pool of appropriately qualified and interested candidates.

Using the 3 x 5 Card-based scorecard to structure situational and behavioral interviews provides a more consistent way to compare candidates, even across more than one interviewer. With every candidate, interviewers should discuss the same five areas that are relevant and important to the open position. Ask candidates to discuss their knowledge and skills as well as positive and negative results in dealing with those areas in their current and prior employment.

I recommend and endorse the methodology outlined in *Topgrading* by Bradford D. Smart, PhD, and also *Who*, a book co-authored by his son, Geoff Smart, and Randy Street. Their methodology greatly enhances your odds of hiring the right candidates and properly onboarding them.

For more detailed interviewing information, see Appendix B.

On day one, during the onboarding process, the new team member should have an opportunity to review the 3 x 5 Card with his or her coach. The new team member has already been indoctrinated regarding the new role from the first time he or she heard about the position, through the interview process, and right up through orientation.

The first day for a newly hired team member should be completely planned and scheduled. Here are some items to consider for such a schedule:

- To welcome the new team member to the organization, have him or her meet with human resources and his or her coach.
- Give the new person a tour of the facility and an introduction to each department.
- Ensure completion of required human resources documents.
- Have the new person lunch with the coach to discuss the 3 x 5 Card for the role.
- Have the new person meet with fellow department members.
- Introduce the new person to the CEO or president.
- Schedule a dinner with the team member and his or her spouse or significant other with the coach and his or her spouse or significant other.

Additionally, prepare the following items in advance of the newly hired team member's first day:

- A designated workspace (office or cubicle) that is fully supplied with pens, paper, and other office tools.
- Set up a telephone extension, e-mail address, and voice-mail box.
- Get business cards printed.
- Any company-provided equipment (e.g., cell phone, laptop, or tablet) should be ordered and delivered to the coach.
- Have benefits-package descriptions and required forms ready at HR.
- Print out operating instructions for the phone system, photocopier, website, intranet, e-mail, voice mail, and so on, and put them on the new hire's desk.
- Do the same with the office layout, including conference rooms, restrooms, and the break room, and provide a company directory.

The first month (at a minimum) should consist of an introduction and orientation to the company and also should be planned in advance. Schedule the new hire for orientation meetings with various departments and even lunch with a teammate or internal customer.

Implement the weekly, monthly, and quarterly meeting rhythms with the new team member immediately. For the first two weeks, though, the coach and team member should meet for a few minutes daily to discuss the prior day's learning and today's expectations.

This is a lot to do and makes the hiring of a new team member seem like a lot of work, but you have only one chance to make a first impression. Make it a *great* one!

The new hire is joining an organization that has delivered from the very beginning a consistent message about expectations and the importance of performance. This should be a welcome difference for most employees and sets your organization apart from all others in the marketplace. There should be no confusion for new team members about their roles or the company's expectations!

If you follow this plan, the odds of your hiring success go up, and the cost of recruiting goes down due to fewer mis-hires.

# CHAPTER 5

# The 3 x 5 Organization Chart

With diligence, over time, you'll have a 3 x 5 card for every member of your organization.

Once the leadership team completes their 3 x 5 Cards, they can start the process with their direct reports and so on down the line until each member of the entire organization has a 3 x 5 Card. Every position will have its top five reasons it gets paid and the performance metrics to accompany each reason.

You can even use your 3 x 5 Cards to help create an organization chart. For example, let's say you have cards for each person in the top three layers of your company. Lay the cards out across a large, open space, such as on the floor or a wall, in an organization-chart format. Peers should be at the same level on the "chart" and their direct reports below them. You'll be missing only the lines that connect people to one another.

Then take a picture of the org chart. That's it. You now have a snapshot of your organization as it exists today. You can see reporting structures as well as the titles and the names of the people occupying each role.

You might even see a 3 x 5 Card without a Post-it Note, signifying an open position.

This is a living org chart, one that is always being updated as changes are made. It's not a static piece of paper in a drawer or a computer file that someone may review only once per year.

Here's an example 3 x 5 Card org chart:

PRESIDENT

Administrative Assistant

LEGAL

IT-IS OFFICER

IT-IS Representatives (4)

VP, FINANCE

CONTROLLER

Director of PURCHASING

PURCHASING Manager

VP, MARKETING

VP, SALES

SALES Representatives (4)

Director of CUSTOMER SERVICE

CUSTOMER SERVICE Representatives (4)

VP, HUMAN RESOURCES

HR Specialists (4)

Director of TRAINING

TRAINING Managers (2)

COO

VP, MANUFACTURING

Director of MANUFACTURING

Director of QUALITY ASSURANCE

Director of INNOVATION

VP, ENGINEERING

Engineers (2)

# CHAPTER 6

# Organization Planning and Growth

Your 3 x 5 Card org chart can help you do some planning for future growth, for both the organization's needs and for individuals' development.

If today your organization does $20 million in revenue and your plan is to double that in the next five years, there are bound to be a few structural changes to the organization, as well as a few people coming and going. There may be some additional people in similar positions, some entirely new positions, and some added coach or leadership positions, but in any case, some change is inevitable.

To make placeholders for these future roles, create 3 x 5 Cards in pastel colors rather than the standard white for existing roles. This makes spotting the new roles on the org chart very easy.

Complete the 3 x 5 Cards for the new positions just as you did for existing roles: Put the job title on the front of the card and the top five reasons the person in that position gets paid on the back. Don't forget to include the performance metrics for each accountability.

Now, one more piece of information needs to be added: When do you anticipate hiring for this role? Put that information underneath the title on the front of the card.

Note: *When* you plan to fill the position should not be a date. It should be the dollar value of revenue that causes the position to be required. For our current example, this could be at $25 or $30 million. Now you know when you should hire this person—when the need is driven by revenue increases, not the calendar.

Take a picture of the future org chart with the cards for anticipated roles in place. That's your snapshot of the organization as it will exist in five years. You can see reporting structures and the titles. But this chart also lets you consider how the people occupying each role can contribute to the organization's future.

Remove all the Post-it Notes from the 3 x 5 Cards for existing roles and think about your people; their current skills; and their ability to grow one, two, or even three levels in the organization. Where do you think each of your current people will be in five years? Place their Post-it Notes on the appropriate 3 x 5 Cards. For each person who has been placed in a position that requires some growth on the employee's part, you can now create a plan for his or her development.

Do not promise any team member a specific future position. You are simply creating a development plan to make your people into more skilled and valuable team members who may provide future growth within the organization.

There may be some team members, though, who do not appear to have growth potential today. How will you provide job enrichment for them to keep them motivated and employed with your organization?

As you develop these growth and enrichment plans, you are creating a learning organization that will be stronger and more competitive than in the past, an organization that will continue to grow as it develops its people.

PRESIDENT

LEGAL

IT-IS OFFICER

IT-IS Representative (4)

VP, FINANCE

CONTROLLER

ACCOUNTANTS (2) $25mm/$30mm

Director of PURCHASING

PURCHASING Manager

PURCHASING Manager $30mm

VP, MARKETING

MARKETING Manager (2)

Director of SALES

SALES Representative (4)

SALES Representative (4) $25mm/$30mm

Director of CUSTOMER SERVICE

CUSTOMER SERVICE Representative (3) / $30mm.

CUSTOMER SERVICE Representative (4)

Administrative Assistant

VP, HUMAN RESOURCES

HR Specialist (4)

Director of TRAINING

TRAINING Manager (2)

TRAINING Manager (2) / $30mm

COO

VP, ENGINEERING

Engineer (2)

Engineer $25mm

Director of INNOVATION

INNOVATION Manager (2) $30mm / $40mm

VP, MANUFACTURING

Director of MANUFACTURING

Director of MANUFACTURING $35mm

Director of QUALITY ASSURANCE

QUALITY ASSURANCE Manager $25mm

# CHAPTER 7

# There Is No *Chapter 7* in the Vocabulary of Most Entrepreneurs

Chapter 7 Bankruptcy is sometimes also called *liquidation bankruptcy*. Firms experiencing this form of bankruptcy are past the stage of reorganization and must sell off any nonexempt assets to pay creditors. In chapter 7, the creditors collect their debts according to how they loaned out the money to the firm (also referred to as the "absolute priority"). A trustee is appointed to ensure that any assets that are secured are sold and that the proceeds are paid to the specific creditors.

For example, secured debt would be loans issued by banks or institutions based upon the value of a specific asset. Whatever assets and residual cash remain after all secured creditors are paid are pooled together to be paid to any outstanding creditors with unsecured loans, such as bondholders and preferred shareholders.

*This definition was adapted from Investopedia.*

# CHAPTER 8

# Implementing 3 x 5 Coaching

I t can be challenging to implement a full 3 x 5 Coaching program. Just the thought of writing the top five reasons each of your direct reports gets paid, plus a metric to measure each of those accountabilities, may seem like a daunting task. However, there is still holding the actual meetings.

Once you make the commitment and tackle the task of filling out the 3 x 5 Cards, some amazing things begin to happen: **You develop clarity around your expectations for the people on your team. They develop clarity around their roles.**

When you hold your first meeting with each team member to discuss the 3 x 5 Cards you each created and agree on a single new 3 x 5 Card, your expectations are aligned, and your relationship is better for having had the conversation.

You can now measure performance against the goals you've mutually set, and so the performance-review process becomes a great discussion that is usually focused on how to improve instead of a debate over the "grade" the employee receives.

Skill development and the team member's personal growth are natural parts of the process as well, because clarity and emphasis on the right goals forces him or her to focus, leading to improved performance. Then performance-review discussions lead to personal-growth conversations and goal setting.

In addition, as roles evolve over time, team members' 3 x 5 Cards need revision, leading to further discussion of roles and goals and deeper relationships.

Finally, when the time comes for a team member to be promoted, the 3 x 5 Card for the new position provides clarity for its accountabilities and necessary skills. The card for the now open position should provide the basis for any advertising done to fill it and serve as the starting point for candidate interview and screening questions.

**Remember that most people quit their coaches, not their company.**

Stop being a manager and become a great coach to retain and grow the people on your team.

The 3 x 5 Card is a simple (though not easy) tool that leads to great coaching.

To get started, first you must complete a 3 x 5 Card for your role with your coach.

Next, explain the 3 x 5 Coach concept to your team. Then share examples of what a completed 3 x 5 Card might look like. (See Appendix A.)

Explain the difference between managing and coaching, the importance of focused accountabilities, and the benefit both the coach and team members will find in reaching a common understanding of their expectations and goals.

*Give your team copies of this book.*

Schedule the initial meeting with each of the team members who report directly to you.

Complete your version of team members' 3 x 5 Cards to prepare for your conversations with them.

Finally, enjoy the conversations!

# CHAPTER 9

# After What Comes How

Once you have an agreed-upon version of each role's 3 x 5 Card, you and your team member have a shared idea of the "what" of the job. It is what the two of you have agreed upon, as well as quantified, in terms of what success looks like.

**Next comes the how: How will the team member accomplish the agreed-upon goals?**

This is where your coaching skills come into play.

An experienced member of the team most likely knows (or can figure out) how to get the job done. Give someone like this room to succeed. Don't micromanage, but do be ready to support him or her. (The word *micro-coach* is not in the dictionary, after all.)

For less experienced members of the team, some guidance may be necessary. Coach them, but allow them to figure it out on their own with your support.

If they tell you they don't know what to do next, then say, "I know you don't know what to do. But if you did know, what would that look like?" You may be surprised at how often someone has an idea of what to do next but is simply afraid to make a mistake.

Human nature is that we are more likely to be committed to our solution than to your solution. But you need to be there to make sure your team members don't fall flat on their faces or waste precious resources in the learning process.

Challenge your team members to spend a few minutes each day thinking about how to do their jobs better. This is not about their to-do lists or reinventing the wheel. Rather, ask them to think about what changes they could make to the process that would improve the end result by saving time and therefore money, improving the product or eliminating mistakes.

This takes their what to a whole new level by thinking about the "how". It also creates a rich environment for discussion between coach and team member.

# CHAPTER 10

# Technology's Impact: Where's the App?

One of the great myths of technology was that it would save time and labor and therefore reduce the length of the workweek.

Technology does save time and labor. It greatly speeds up processes. But this has meant only that we do more in the same amount of time. With all of the productivity gains through technology, expectations have risen at an even faster pace, and so employers expect greater levels of performance than ever before. The workweek has not gotten any shorter and, in fact, is often longer than it once was.

We are connected twenty-four seven, and people want (but think they need) answers immediately. We live in a world of instant gratification, fast decisions, multiple options, immediate reaction, and ever-increasing expectations. All this may be good for business but not necessarily for the individuals working in it.

Here is a simple real-world example to illustrate the pace of change.

In 1985, I was a marketing director for Burger King Corporation. If I wanted the advertising agency to do something for the company, I would write a letter by hand on a legal pad and then put it in my desk drawer for a day.

Then I would take it out and reread it, making any final edits or changes, and then give it to my secretary—the title *administrative assistant* had not yet been coined—to type. Yes, *type* on an IBM Selectric typewriter, using carbon paper so we could keep a copy for our files while we mailed the original to the agency.

The post office would deliver the letter three or four days later, and then the folks at the advertising agency would read it; think about their response; and repeat the writing, editing, typing, and mailing process to get it to me.

All this took about two weeks. It required lead time, planning, and thinking.

Today, I would bang out an e-mail in a few seconds (or maybe minutes) and hit send. The agency would read it, bang out a reply, and hit send. All this activity would take ten to fifteen minutes.

The editing and thinking time has been compressed, but this does not necessarily lead to productivity or even efficiency. Instead, it usually leads to rework.

Now, 3 x 5 Coaching puts the editing and thinking time back into the process of coaching and leading people.

Technology has allowed for rapid increases in doing, but human nature does not change that fast. A successful coach recognizes the need for clarity, consistency, direction, and support that people want and need.

If you are looking for a shortcut to this process or a 3 x 5 application to make it easier, there isn't one. That is on purpose.

The key is for each person to spend some time thinking and then writing; then they get together to discuss and agree on the direction so that both parties are on the same page.

# CHAPTER 11

# Entrepreneurs Never Want to Think about Chapter 11

C hapter 11 Bankruptcy can also be called *rehabilitation bankrupt-cy*. It's much more involved than Chapter 7, as it allows the firm the opportunity to reorganize its debt and try to reemerge as a healthy organization. What this means is that the firm will contact its creditors in an attempt to change the terms on loans, such as the interest rate and dollar value of payments. Like its cousin, chapter 11 requires that a trustee be appointed; however, rather than selling off all assets to pay back creditors, the trustee supervises the debtor's assets and allows the business to continue. It's important to note that debt is not absolved in chapter 11: the restructuring changes only the terms of the debt, and the firm must continue to pay it back through future earnings.

If a company is successful in chapter 11, it will typically be expected to continue operating in an efficient manner with its newly structured debt. If it is not successful, then it will file for chapter 7 and liquidate. In both instances, common shareholders most likely will see little (if any) return on their investments.

This definition was adapted from Investopedia.

# CHAPTER 12

# Execution Excellence

I've noted that the 3 x 5 Card is the what of a position. It defines why a person gets paid to do that work and the performance metrics for each of the accountabilities.

Every quarter, the organization has a new set of goals, and each team member may be responsible for some of the activity to achieve those goals. The expectations for a team member most likely will not change radically every quarter, but there may be some additional or adjusted priorities or changes in circumstance.

Naturally, the team member focuses his or her daily work on the top five reasons the position gets paid and on his or her most recently defined priorities. But then the coach drops by and asks the team member to take on an additional task. What does the team member do?

With the 3 x 5 Card specifying why he or she gets paid in one hand and a list of quarterly priorities in the other, which hand should the team member use to pick up a new task, duty, or priority? He or she does not have a free hand or free time.

How do the department's and his or her individual priorities support and drive the organization's priorities and goals?

The department should be measured by a few key metrics (KPIs) that tell the story of its performance and provide focus. What are they? And what are the KPIs applied to the team member's performance?

The department should have one key priority for the quarter (and, if necessary, two or three supporting priorities). What is it?

The team member should have no more than five priorities for the quarter. What are they?

If the team member accomplishes his or her priorities and achieves the KPIs and the department achieves the same for its own, the organization should have a good chance for success. The only way for a team member to take on more and keep some semblance of a reasonable workweek is to determine where the new task, duty, or priority fits into his or her job function (why he or she gets paid) or current priorities. If it supersedes one of these, it is time to consider what should be delegated to another capable member of the team or what can be shifted to a later date to allow for this change of priorities.

The coach and team member should have an honest conversation about revising the team member's job functions (and therefore his or her position's 3 x 5 Card) or current priorities. Here, the coach may have to recommend a course of action. (This should not happen very often.)

Next, translate the new priority into the set of component tasks required to complete it. It may take five tasks or even twenty-five. Each task should be broken down into bite-size pieces—something that can be accomplished in forty-five to sixty minutes of uninterrupted work time. The block of time for each task should be scheduled on the team member's calendar.

As an example, if one task is estimated at three hours to complete, then four discrete forty-five-minute work segments (or three one-hour segments) are then scheduled. **Once a task is on the calendar, each team member must respect his or her time and get the work done.**

Every employee should treat these work segments as high priority, not something that can be put off or skipped. You wouldn't skip or arbitrarily move a meeting with your team member, coach, or the company president, so don't do that with these work segments.

In addition, these are to be uninterrupted periods of work. Forty-five to sixty minutes is long enough to make real progress on a task but not so long for someone to be out of reach that it disrupts the team's workflow.

The employee should close his or her door, find a small office somewhere in the building, or hang a sign outside his or her cubicle. He or she should turn off the ringer on his or her phone(s) and the chime on his or her e-mail and should avoid any other distractions.

- At forty-five minutes each, three work segments per day is only two hours and fifteen minutes of focused work time.
- With three work segments per day (each at forty-time minutes), an employee has 180 work segments per quarter.
- There are typically twenty working days in a month (excluding holidays, weekends, and vacation days), so an employee has about sixty days per quarter to accomplish his or her goals.

How many forty-five-minute work segments do the tasks that make up your quarterly priorities require? Use the formula below:

- Priorities x Tasks x Forty-five-minute segments = Time required to complete your priorities

For example, if you had five priorities with only six tasks per priority and only six segments of forty-five minutes for each task, that equals 135 hours over thirteen weeks. This means that more than ten hours per week must be dedicated to those five priorities!

Remember, rarely do we accomplish as much as we think we can in the allotted time. Now you know why. It is no wonder that we feel stressed.

**Manage your time wisely. Treat it as the most precious resource you have, because it is.**

From time to time, the organization's goals or direction may even change, requiring some changes for team members within the company. If this happens, then it is time to review the 3 x 5 Card and anyone affected by those changes should ask himself or herself a few questions:

- Are the goals still **realistic**, given the changes in resources or direction?
- Are they still **timely**? Is it still the right time to achieve them?
- Are they still **relevant**? Do they still align with the company's strategy?

If a change to one or more of the priorities is appropriate, repeat the steps you took to develop the original set of priorities to revise the priority list.

# CHAPTER 13

# Calendar Management

Here are some simple actions for creating the discipline of good calendar management.

Start each morning by spending five minutes reviewing your planned accomplishments, and close each day by spending ten minutes reviewing your accomplishments and planning for tomorrow.

Have planned time to work with no interruptions every day. In the previous chapter, there was an example of three forty-five-minute work segments planned per day. This only amounts to two and one-quarter hours per day to work on your priorities, leaving plenty of time for meetings, e-mail, voice mail, and all the other things you need to fit into your schedule.

Close your door or hang a Do Not Disturb note outside your cubicle. Turn off the telephone's ringer, and turn off all beeps or chimes for e-mail or voice mail. *Focus!*

Do not attend meetings that do not have a written purpose, expected outcomes, and decisions to be made. You should also receive an agenda with timelines and a list of attendees.

In meetings, phones and e-mail should be off. If you are going to be in a meeting, then **be there**. If there is associated reading material, prereading is always preferable to reading documents to one another in the meeting. Always request to preread.

Meetings should start on time and end on time.

For any department or team invited to a meeting, find out who really needs to be there, and have only those people attend.

Keep the meeting focused on the purpose, outcomes, and decisions to be made. Don't let it wander off course or drag on.

This approach to meetings will ruffle a few feathers in your company at first, but if everyone treats meetings this way, the organization will be much more productive.

**Schedule some fun outside of work every week.** Don't leave it to happenstance; this is how burnout happens. Put fun activities, such as date night or attending a movie, play, sporting event, or concert, into your calendar. Make time for family activities and time with friends.

### ~~Management~~ >Coaching

- Stop managing and start coaching.
- All meetings with your team should be short, positive, and impactful—weekly, monthly, and in between.
- Make sure that one-on-one time with your team members is included on your calendar, and treat that time as the most important meeting of the day. Be there.
- Provide ongoing updates and feedback to your team. You cannot *overcommunicate*.

**Make sure you have a few open windows on your calendar every week.** No matter how hard we try, we cannot anticipate everything. Leave some time free for unexpected e-mails and calls, both incoming and outgoing, as well as impromptu meetings.

**Respect your time and calendar, and others will too.** If you make yourself always available by constantly adjusting your calendar, people will not respect your time.

Scheduled meetings (one-on-one or for a group) are a commitment of your most precious resource—your time. Treat it that way.

Too many people think they are busy at work because their schedules are filled with meetings. **Remember that meetings do not equal work. Meetings are only time spent. Productive activity equals work.**

So if a meeting produces some tangible result that you contributed to, then you were working. But if the meeting *doesn't* produce a meaningful result, then that meeting was not work. Worse yet, **if you were at the meeting and made no contribution, then you were just a spectator.**

# CHAPTER 14

# Personal Development

Schedule time in your calendar each week to *read* (A-level players read at least twenty-four books per year), *learn* (gain new knowledge), and *grow* (improve existing skills). Whether during the workday, in the evening, or on the weekend, reading plays a critical part in your personal development.

**Start by asking yourself, "What are my strengths?"** *StrengthsFinder 2.0* is a wonderful book by Tom Rath that can help you discover your top five strengths and build a plan to improve them.

The premise of the book is that we all have certain areas of strength and other areas where we are not as strong. In business, it is best to work to improve your strengths and hire others to offset areas where you are not strong. The author has developed thirty-four themes and ideas for action. You simply read the book, take an online assessment, and receive a personalized report on your top five areas of strength. You can then develop a plan to improve your strengths (also done online). Each team member should develop an action plan to improve strengths with his or her coach and be accountable for executing against that plan.

Look for opportunities to help yourself, your team members, and your colleagues to grow.

Consider making some of the following ideas part of your own action plan:

- **Create a company library.** Make it easy for people to read business books and trade journals. Remember that the purpose of a library is for people to borrow and read, so new books are not necessary. Gently used books will do just fine. The company can buy these inexpensively on the Internet.
- **Start or join a breakfast club.** Enjoy a coffee-and-education group with like-minded individuals from your company or industry or others you know.
- Take advantage of the many instructional videos, TED Talks, and other resources available on the Internet.
- **Know your industry and the world of business.** Read your industry's trade publications. Become the go-to person for information. Read local, national, and international business publications.
- **Be a lifelong learner.** Take college courses whether they relate to your field or not. Education never hurts your personal development. Participate in webinars and listen to podcasts that interest you.

Your opportunities for growth and learning are limitless. The key to success is building a plan and then making the time to accomplish its goals. Don't procrastinate. Get started today!

# APPENDIX A

# 3 x 5 Cards for Key Roles

## SAMPLE ACCOUNTABILITIES

Below is a list of potential "reasons people get paid" based on the variety of disciplines in an organization. Every organization has its own idiosyncrasies; therefore, this is not a one-size-fits-all list. Rather, it's merely a starting point to help you develop your organization's 3 x 5 Cards.

The specific titles have been left out, but in each case, the assumption is that the role shown is for a **senior-level person who leads the discipline.**

The staff reporting to the senior leader might have some of the same accountabilities but also a few that are different based on level and role within the organization.

It is important to note that all accountabilities should be measured, whether in dollars, with percentages, or by timeliness. If something can't be measured, then it is most likely a task to be done and not at the level of an accountability.

Also, do not just make a list of tasks, no matter how important they may seem to be. As an example, when asked to do this exercise, most financial people write things like "Publish the monthly financial reports by the fifteenth of next month." It is important and measurable, so it must be an accountability, right?

While it is important that the reports be published and it's nice to have them by the fifteenth, that does not make them an accountability. It is far more important that the reports are accurate and usable and that they provide guidance for improved future performance.

So ask yourself this: What does a person in a particular role contribute to the success of the organization? Which of his or her contributions are the most important, and how do we measure the impact of those contributions?

That is why we put "Why do you get paid?" at the top of the backside of the 3 x 5 Card.

- **How exactly do you earn your paycheck?** In other words...
- **What is the real purpose of your role?** In other words...
- **What is the real value that your position brings to the organization?**

Once you have settled on the top five reasons, then the measurements can usually be best determined by another simple question: "How do you know if you are doing a good job?"

As the leader of the organization, start with yourself. Create a 3 x 5 Card for your position and find someone else to do one for you as well, whether it is a board of directors, your executive coach, or maybe someone from a professional organization you belong to who knows you well.

Now, have a one-on-one with your "coach" to finalize your 3 x 5 Card.

Next, move on to the leadership team. As the organization's leader, complete your direct reports' 3 x 5 Cards first and have your one-on-one meetings to finalize their cards with you as their coach. Then it is time to cascade the process through the rest of the organization.

It will take a while for some people to grasp the concept of accountabilities versus tasks. It will also be a challenge for some people to limit themselves to only five accountabilities. By far the most challenging part, though, is quantifying or measuring performance.

Many times I have been told, "You don't understand. My position is unique, and most of what I do can't be measured."

My response is direct and simple: "What would you say if I told you, 'If there are no KPIs, there is no job'?" This usually causes people to rethink their "it can't be measured" position and, amazingly, come up with a few good ways to document performance.

Stick with it. Almost everything any of us do can be defined in a way that allows for KPIs to be developed.

PRESIDENT / OWNER

## WHY DO YOU GET PAID?

- "A" Players on the Leadership Team     +75 percent*
- Net Cash Flow     $500k / 10 percent
- Return on Investment (or Assets)     12 percent
- Brand Promise Delivery
  - Net Promoter Score     60
  - Repeat Customers     +95 percent**
- Leadership Team Development Plans     100 percent***

* The goal would be to have at least 75 percent of the Leadership Team be considered "A" players.

** The goal is to have at least 95 percent of existing customers become repeat buyers.

*** The goal is to have individual development plans in place for 100 percent of the leadership team members.

OPERATIONS LEADER

---

WHY DO YOU GET PAID?

- Gross margin                                  55 percent
- "A" Players Retained                          95 percent
- Internal Hires for Open Positions             50 percent*
- Customer Visits per Quarter                   13
- Operations Team Development Plans             100 percent of team

---

* The goal would be to have at least 50 percent of the open positions in the company filled by internal candidates.

FINANCIAL LEADER

WHY DO YOU GET PAID?

- Return on Invested Dollars — 12 percent
- Accurate Budget Forecasts — ± 2.5 percent
- Accounts Receivable Days — < 30*
- Financial Literacy of Leadership Team — 100 percent of team**
- Financial Team Development Plans — 100 percent of team

\* The goal would be to have accounts receivable at less than thirty days on average.

\*\* The goal is to have the entire leadership team become financially conversant with the P&L, balance sheet, cash flow, and other key metrics.

MARKETING LEADER

---

WHY DO YOU GET PAID?

- Leads Generated                 100 / month
- Brand Awareness             >73 percent
- Promotion Effectiveness / ROI     +12 percent
- Trade Show ROI              +12 percent
- Marketing Team Development Plans    100 percent of team

SALES LEADER

WHY DO YOU GET PAID?

- Leads Converted                                     25 / month
- Revenue Growth (New & Existing Clients)   +15 percent
- Sales Efficiency Ratio                           $15.00/$1.00*
- Market Share Growth                           +5 percent
- Sales Team Development Plans               100 percent of team

\* Sales Efficiency Ratio is measured by how many dollars of contribution margin are generated for every dollar of the sales team's salary.

HUMAN RESOURCES LEADER

## WHY DO YOU GET PAID?

- Regrettable Turnover      < 1 percent*
- Open Positions      < 5 percent
- Management Efficiency Ratio      $10.00/$1.00**
- Employee Net Promoter Score      50
- HR Team Development Plans      100 percent of team

* Regrettable Turnover is the percentage of people who leave the organization but whom you did not want to lose.

** Management Efficiency Ratio is measured by how many contribution-margin dollars are generated for every dollar of the management team's salary.

MANUFACTURING LEADER

## WHY DO YOU GET PAID?

- Gross / Contribution Margin — 58 percent / 42 percent
- Labor Efficiency Ratio — $3.25/$1.00*
- Machine Utilization Rate — 65 percent
- Days Lost Due to Injury — 0 days
- Manufacturing Team Development Plans — 100 percent of team

* Labor Efficiency Ratio is measured by how many gross-margin dollars are generated for every dollar of direct-labor salary.

THE 3X5 COACH

LEGAL LEADER

## WHY DO YOU GET PAID?

- Corporate Legal Compliance                         100 percent
- Legal Budget Management                           ± 5 percent
- Litigation Win Rate                                      +90 percent
- Employee Policy Signatures/Communication    100 percent
- Legal Team Development Plans                      100 percent of team

INNOVATION LEADER

## WHY DO YOU GET PAID?

- Products Developed on Time                 ± 1 week
- Products Developed on Budget               ± 2.5 percent
- First Year New Product Market Share        20 percent
- Accurate Product Market Forecasts          ± 5 percent
- Innovation Team Development Plans          100 percent of team

PURCHASING / SUPPLY CHAIN LEADER

---

WHY DO YOU GET PAID?

- Reduction in Cost of Goods Sold                 5 percent
- Days Lost Due to Product Shortage               0
- Supplier Quality Ratings                        +90 percent
- Material Quality Specifications                 100 percent
- Purchasing/Supply Team Development Plans        100 percent of team

QUALITY ASSURANCE LEADER

WHY DO YOU GET PAID?

| | |
|---|---|
| ▪ QA Standards Compliance | 100 percent |
| ▪ OSHA Compliance | 100 percent |
| ▪ Product Defect Rate | ± 2 percent |
| ▪ Environmental Compliance | 100 percent |
| ▪ Quality Assurance Team Development Plans | 100 percent of team |

TRAINING LEADER

WHY DO YOU GET PAID?

- New Employees Trained / Quarter 125
- Current Employees Trained / Quarter 200
- Training Net Promoter Score 75
- Training Capacity Used +80 percent
- Training Team Development Plans 100 percent of team

CUSTOMER SERVICE LEADER

WHY DO YOU GET PAID?

- Customer Retention                          95 percent
- Customer Issues Resolved on Phone           75 percent
- Top Five Issues Occurrence Reduction        10 percent each
- Operations Training for Key Issues          100 percent
- Customer Service Development Plans          100 percent of team

ENGINEERING LEADER

## WHY DO YOU GET PAID?

- Product Designs on Time                    ± 1 week
- Product Designs on Budget                   ± 2.5 percent
- Engineering Net Promoter Score              75
- Energy Consumption Reduction                5 percent
- Engineering Team Development Plans          100 percent of team

IT/IS LEADER

WHY DO YOU GET PAID?

- System Uptime                    99.75 percent
- Reduction in IT/IS Costs         5 percent
- IT/IS Net Promoter Score         75
- Issue Resolution Time            24 hours
- IT/IS Team Development Plans     100 percent of team

# APPENDIX B

# The Job Interview

*W*ho, by Geoff Smart and Randy Street, contains some of the best interviewing techniques. I highly recommend you read it and adopt their methodology for recruiting and interviewing.

The authors outline four types of interview: the Screening Interview, the Topgrading Interview, the Focused Interview, and the Reference Interview.

**The Screening Interview** is designed to quickly cull the candidate list down to the most qualified individuals. Ask the following questions of each candidate:

- What are your career goals?
- What are you really good at professionally?
- What are you not good at or not interested in doing professionally?
- Who were your last five bosses, and how will each rate your performance on a scale of one to ten when we talk to them?

The **Topgrading Interview** is a much longer, face-to-face interview designed to discuss the candidate's history from high school through his or her current job. For *every* job the person has held, ask the following questions:

- What were you hired to do?
- What accomplishments are you proudest of?
- What were some low points during that job?
- Who were the people you worked with?
- What was it like working for your boss?
- When I speak with him or her, what will he or she tell me your biggest strengths and areas for improvement were?
- How would you rate the team you inherited on an A, B, or C scale?
- What changes did you make? Did you hire anybody? Fire anybody?
- How would you rate the team you left on an A, B, or C scale?
- Why did you leave that job?

The **Focused Interview** is about the outcomes and competencies listed on the scorecard for the position. For each of the key outcomes and competencies of the position, ask the following questions:

- What were your biggest accomplishments in this area during your career?
- What are your insights into your biggest mistakes and lessons learned in this area?

The **Reference Interview** is intended to corroborate what you have heard during the first three interviews with the candidate. Of every boss the candidate has worked for during the last ten years, ask the following questions:

- In what context did you work with the candidate?
- What were his or her biggest strengths?
- What were his or her biggest areas for improvement back then?
- How would you rate his/her overall performance in that job on a scale of zero to ten?
- What about his or her performance causes you to give that rating?
- The candidate mentioned that he or she struggled with _____ in their job. Can you tell me more about that?

By having a scripted plan for interviewing candidates, you greatly improve your odds of success, because you cover the same areas with each candidate and leave out nothing about any of them.

When the questions are the same, it is also much easier to compare candidates.

When you are using several interviewers, a list of consistent questions makes it much easier for them to rate candidates, as they know every interviewer covered the same areas.

*Adapted from the book.*

# About the Author

D ave Baney is the founder and CEO of 55 Questions LLC. He works with successful top executives who have a driving ambition to crush their competition. He is an experienced, strategic marketer who enables leaders of growth-challenged organizations to achieve their aspirations.

Dave works with entrepreneurs and CEOs of growth companies and their leadership teams in the implementation of Scaling Up and the Four Decisions. He provides executive-team coaching and development as well as strategic planning, accountability workshops, and keynote speaking.

Dave brings thirty-plus years of leadership and management experience to his company. He is a multidisciplined executive with extensive experience working in the United States, Latin America, and Europe. He has led teams at Burger King Corporation and McDonald's Corporation as a senior executive in the disciplines of marketing, operations, new-product development, and real estate and construction.

Throughout his career, Dave has provided coaching and counseling to hundreds of small-to-midsize entrepreneurs and franchise business owners in more than fifty industries.

Dave and his wife are former residents of Chicago; Miami; and Milan, Italy. They now live in Las Vegas. Dave is an avid golfer, and he enjoys travel, reading, and learning.

# About 55 Questions LLC

## Courage To Set The Bar High Starts With A Clear Path.

A CEO can't keep tabs on every aspect of the company. After all, that's why you hire people. But the organizational chart may lack clarity, which leads to missed opportunities and unnecessary impediments. (Titles are not to-do lists.)

Founded by Dave Baney, 55 Questions is a discovery process to help CEOs and their management teams create a clear picture of their business's current state, determine the daunting but attainable goals for growth, and shape the path to reach that destination.

Using a direct questioning method (sometimes uncomfortably direct), Dave will lead you to a better understanding of your company's landscape from both a bird's-eye and worm's-eye view. There will be accountability where things now fall through cracks. That cluttered growth plan will become simplified, delineated, and effective.

## Accountability Drives Action.

55 Questions incorporates several unique processes from the Gazelles International Coaches growth method, which focuses on helping executive teams make the right choices when it comes to the Four Decisions: People, Strategy, Execution, and Cash.

At 55 Questions, we look for answers in these areas to help you get your leadership team on the same page, freeing up your day and turning accountability into standard operating procedure.

CEOs are able to streamline processes by getting to the nuts and bolts of what needs to be done through leadership-team accountability. This energizes the company, drives priorities, and cuts through bureaucratic clutter.

The influence from Gazelles is one part of what makes 55 Questions such an effective game changer for CEOs and their leadership teams, as are *3 x 5 Coaching* and *The Cash Flow Story*.

ANSWERS GROW YOUR BUSINESS
www.55questions.com

# Notes